PRAYERS FOR YOUR ADULT CHILDREN

A Thirty-Day Devotional

Lisa Hodgins

WESTBOW
PRESS®
A DIVISION OF THOMAS NELSON
& ZONDERVAN

Scripture quotations marked (NIV) are taken from the Holy Bible, New International Version®, NIV®. Copyright © 1973, 1978, 1984, 2011 by Biblica, Inc.™ Used by permission of Zondervan. All rights reserved worldwide. www.zondervan.com The "NIV" and "New International Version" are trademarks registered in the United States Patent and Trademark Office by Biblica, Inc.™

Scripture quotations are taken from the Holy Bible, New Living Translation, copyright ©1996, 2004, 2007, 2013, 2015 by Tyndale House Foundation. Used by permission of Tyndale House Publishers, Inc., Carol Stream, Illinois 60188. All rights reserved.

WestBow Press books may be ordered through booksellers or by contacting:

WestBow Press
A Division of Thomas Nelson & Zondervan
1663 Liberty Drive
Bloomington, IN 47403
www.westbowpress.com
1 (866) 928-1240

Because of the dynamic nature of the Internet, any web addresses or links contained in this book may have changed since publication and may no longer be valid. The views expressed in this work are solely those of the author and do not necessarily reflect the views of the publisher, and the publisher hereby disclaims any responsibility for them.

Any people depicted in stock imagery provided by Thinkstock are models, and such images are being used for illustrative purposes only.
Certain stock imagery © Thinkstock.

ISBN: 978-1-5127-9840-1 (sc)
ISBN: 978-1-5127-9841-8 (e)

Library of Congress Control Number: 2017911917

Print information available on the last page.

WestBow Press rev. date: 09/15/2017

CONTENTS

INTRODUCTION

The *illusion* is that when you have a child you will love them, raise them right, and after high school they will go to college, get a job, live independently, and get married. You can then enjoy your life surrounded by a wonderfully-large family of kids, spouses and grandchildren without any more worries.

The *reality* is that we live in a fallen, sinful world. There may be many happy, memorable times parents of adult children experience while watching their children live out their lives. However, too many parents experience difficult and painful times as they watch their children make bad choices with devastating consequences.

We are not perfect people. We are not immune to making bad choices. We struggle with our own choices and the consequences of those choices every day. Our children will do the same. It is human nature. With each generation, we are seeing our society getting further and further away from God and his values. From early childhood, our children are bombarded with worldly things and Satan's schemes to draw them away from God.

Is there hope? YES! Can their lives be changed? YES! But not by you; that's God's job! Change can come about and God can use you, if you are willing. How does God use us to reach our adult children who don't know God or who have strayed from their godly upbringing? He uses us primarily through prayer and by our own godly example of living and loving. While that sounds very simplified, it's a life-long practice with eternal rewards. (Isaiah 40:31; NLT) reads "...but those who hope in the Lord will renew their strength. They will soar on wings like eagles; they will run and not grow weary; they will walk and not be faint." Never underestimate the power of God and his ability to reach the lost.

What if we made lots of mistakes raising our kids, or we weren't living for God at the time we raised them? What about those times we were not being a godly example? It doesn't matter. God knows this and still has a plan for them. God wants to provide our kids with even more blessings than we could imagine or ever wish for them. Our God can restore broken hearts, broken relationships and even broken dreams. Our God can heal our hurts as well as theirs. (Revelation 21:5; NLT) states, "He who was seated on the throne said, 'I am making everything new!' Then he said, 'Write this down, for these words are trustworthy and true.'" Our God can make all things new.

You will find at the bottom of each page a **Mediation Moments** section. Don't just read the page and walk away. Ask God to show you what he wants you to learn from each lesson. This section is where you record what specifically touched your heart in that devotional. What lesson did you learn? How can you apply it to your life?

Let's start the journey of prayer for our adult children. Hold on to God's promises from his word, watch as God does his marvelous work in loving our adult children, healing and restoring relationships, while drawing them closer to him. You can leave your children legacies of money or things, but none is as valuable as leaving them a spiritual legacy.

Yes, there is hope. God holds it in his hand and he is holding his hand out to you.

CHOICES

If you think back to when you were a young adult, I'm sure we can all think of times in our lives when we made poor choices. That is just what it was--your choice. God gave all of us free will. So how do we stand by and watch our children make destructive choices that affect not just them, but all those around them: spouses, children, friends, parents and co-workers.

We can try talking, yelling, crying, guilt, or bargaining, but it probably won't work. Change has to come from the heart. We can't change their hearts; only God can. (Deuteronomy 30:6; NLT) "The Lord your God will change your heart and the hearts of all your descendants, so that you will love him with all your heart and soul and so you may live!"

So, what can we do? Start by praying and learning the many promises God has given us in his Word. Not sure how to pray? Review the sample prayer at the end of each page to help you get started. God loves them and wants to restore them. He sees exactly what is going on in their lives and loves them anyway. (Isaiah 54:13; NLT) "I will teach all your children, and they will enjoy great peace." We serve a mighty God who has put the sun and moon in the sky, created the earth, parted the seas, tells the wind where to go, and yet speaks to us in a small, still voice. Listen for his voice. He will guide you. As we learn to turn over to him our fears, hurts, and doubts, we will find our joy and peace returning. (Psalms 46:10; NLT) Be still, and know that I am God!" God hears your prayers. Rest in him. You will see change, but it may just start in you.

> While your adult children are making their choices, we can make our own.
>
> Instead of Worry, I **choose** to Trust God to give them wisdom to make right choices.
>
> Instead of Fear, I **choose** to have Faith that God is working for their good.
>
> Instead of Anger, I **choose** to show Love, by my words and actions.

1

Instead of Nagging or Complaining, I **choose** to Listen more and talk less.

Instead trying to Fix the problem, I **choose** to Let Go and Let God do His work.

What choices can you make today to turn the situation over to God? Here is a great quote from Joyce Meyers: "Help them be all they can be, not what we want them to be."

(Proverbs 3:5-6; NLT) "Trust in the Lord with all your heart; do not depend on your own understanding. Seek his will in all you do, and he will show you which path to take."

(Romans 8:28; NLT) "And we know that God causes everything to work together for the good of those who love God and are called according to his purpose for them."

(Deuteronomy 10:12; NLT) "And now, Israel, what does the Lord your God require of you? He requires only that you fear the Lord your God, and live in a way that pleases him, and love him and serve him with all your heart and soul."

(John 15:16; NLT) "You didn't choose me. I chose you. I appointed you to go and produce lasting fruit, so that the Father will give you whatever you ask for, using my name."

Prayer: Lord, I pray for my children. Give them wisdom to make right choices. Help them to have a deeper understanding of who you are and how great your love is for them. Surround them with godly people to encourage and inspire them to live for you. When they make wrong choices, show them how to turn it around and make it right. Be glorified in their lives. I choose to trust you with my children. I choose not to worry but to find rest in your promises. Thank you for your endless love for us.

Meditation Moments:

_____

_____

_____

_____

_____

_____

_____

_____

COMFORT

Have you ever wondered what would happen if God took you home today? Who would be praying for your children? Who would love them like you? Jesus! He gave his life for them. In (Deuteronomy 31:6b; NIV), He promised, "...Never will I leave you." We have the faith to believe that for ourselves, but do you have the faith to know that verse applies to them as well? The definition of faith is "complete trust or confidence in someone or something."

Were your children saved at a young age and now aren't walking with the Lord? God called our children holy while they were living with us. Does God love them any less now? Of course not. He is still at work in their lives, even though we don't see it with our natural eyes.

> (I Corinthians 7:14; NIV) "For the unbelieving husband has been sanctified through his wife, and the unbelieving wife has been sanctified through her believing husband. Otherwise your children would be unclean, but as it is, they are holy." God will continue to work in their lives. He loves them more than we do. You can be assured God is working in their life. Your prayers and godly example of love will help them see what living for God looks like."

> (Philippians 1:6; NIV) "...being confident of this, that he who began a good work in you will carry it on to completion until the day of Christ Jesus." It says to be confident. Trust God who is able to do more than we can imagine.

> (Ephesians 3:20; NIV) "Now to him who is able to do immeasurably more than all we ask or imagine, according to his power that is at work in us" It's pretty exciting to think God can do more than we can even imagine. He loves them and has great plans for them and for us.

> (Jeremiah 29:11; NLT) "For I know the plans I have for you,' says the Lord. 'They are plans for good and not for disaster, to give you a future and a hope.'"

What if your children never accepted Jesus as their Lord and Savior? Don't be discouraged. God's desire is that all men would be saved.

> (I Timothy 2:4; NIV) "[God]who wants all people to be saved and to come to a knowledge of the truth…"

> (Psalms 119:50; NLT) "Your promises revive me; it comforts me in all my troubles."

> (Psalms 94:19; NLT) "When doubts filled my mind, your comfort gave me renewed hope and cheer."

> (II Corinthians 1:4; (NLT) "He comforts us in all our troubles so that we can comfort others. When they are troubled, we will be able to give them the same comfort God has given us."

> (Hebrews 4:16; NIV) "Let us then approach God's throne of grace with confidence, so that we may receive mercy and find grace to help us in our time of need."

Prayer: Thank you for being our great comforter. You dry our tears and lift our weary heads when we are full of sorrow. Thank you for your promise of salvation through your son Jesus. Thank you for the work you are doing in my children's lives, even if I can't see it. I will trust your word that promises you are able to do more than I can even imagine. Thank you for your amazing love for us and giving us comfort through your word and others.

Meditation Moments:

COPING

When your adult children are living destructive lifestyles or just making some poor choices, how do you deal with it? What I've learned, and continue to learn, is to hang on to the promises of God for us. (Isaiah 54:10; NLT) states, "For the mountains may move and the hills disappear, but even then my faithful love for you will remain. My covenant of blessing will never be broken, says the Lord, who has mercy on you." Our God is merciful and will help you cope during these difficult times. (Romans 2:4; NLT) says, "Don't you see how wonderfully kind, tolerant, and patient God is with you? Does this mean nothing to you? Can't you see that his kindness is intended to turn you from your sin?" Aren't you glad God is patient with us? He is patient and tolerant with our kids too. God is more than able to use the journey they are on now to teach them life lessons and to turn them away from sin. Ask God to help you be patient while he is working in their lives.

Remember that he loves them more than we do. No matter how far away they seem from God, He is right there with them. He is right there with you too. We have God's promises to carry us and help us cope when discouragement surrounds us. Be comforted in knowing God is present. He will restore your joy. Find your rest in him and his Word.

(Isaiah 49:17 –18; NLT) "Soon your descendants will come back, and all who are trying to destroy you will go away. Look around you and see, for all your children will come back to you. As surely as I live, says the Lord, they will be like jewels or bridal ornaments for you to display."

(Isaiah 49:16; NLT) "See, I have written your [their] name in the palms of my hands..."

(Isaiah 49:23b; NLT) "Those who trust in me will never be put to shame."

(Isaiah 40:31; NIV) "But those who hope in the Lord will renew their strength. They will soar on wings like eagles; they will run and not grow weary; they will walk and not be faint."

Prayer: Lord, my heart is hurting and sometimes I don't know how to cope with all that is happening in my life and my family. Give me the wisdom to know what steps I can take. Guide me according to your will and plan for me. I thank you for your promises. I can be confident you will bring my children back to you. Thank you for loving them more than me. Thank you for loving us all so intimately that our names are written on your palms. Thank you, Lord, for easing my fears. I know I can cope because of your promises. I am confident that I will not be put to shame because my trust is in you.

Meditation Moments:

_____

_____

_____

_____

_____

_____

_____

_____

_____

_____

DISTANCE

As parents, you have probably had experiences where you were distant from your children. You may have been there physically, but you were emotionally absent. Sometimes we get so wrapped up in ourselves, or we get so exhausted or so busy, that we are not mentally available when our kids need us. Maybe you have experienced times when you should have distanced yourself from them and didn't. You enabled instead of promoting independence. In either case, finding the right distance can be an important decision to make.

As our children go through struggles of their own, they may need you to be available to them to provide wisdom, encouragement, inspiration, or to just quietly listen. Or, you may have to step back and distance yourself, allowing them to make their own decisions, even if it's not how you would handle the situation. In *Luke 15*, the father of the prodigal son didn't go chasing after his child. When the son returned home, the father was filled with love and compassion and welcomed him. God can show you what changes you can make to either distance yourself or be available for your children. (Proverbs 1:5; NIV) "Let the wise listen and add to their learning, and let the discerning get guidance."

We want our children to make the right choices, however, it's important to allow them the freedom to make mistakes and hopefully learn from those mistakes. That will help them develop into responsible adults and not be co-dependent on others. I was advised by a wise counselor not to interfere with my adult children's lives unless they asked me for advice. I had to learn to step back and let them be. That turned out to be the best advice I could have received. I had to learn to listen more and talk less. It was incredibly difficult, but was worth the effort. It gave me more peace and our relationships improved. That was the best result I could have imagined. Learning to listen more and talk less is a great lesson for any relationship.

(James 1:19; NIV) "My dear brothers and sisters, take note of this: Everyone should be quick to listen, slow to speak and slow to become angry."

(Psalms 85:8; NIV) "I will listen to what God the Lord says; he promises peace to his people, his faithful servants—but let them not turn to folly."

(Proverbs 3:7; NIV*)* "Don't be wise in your own eyes; instead fear the Lord and shun evil."

(Romans 8:31; NIV*)* "What, then, shall we say in response to these things? If God is for us, who can be against us?"

Prayer: Lord, thank you for my children and for the work you are doing in their lives. Give them wisdom in the choices they make. Help me to be strong in your word so I can offer them wisdom when they ask or encourage them when they need it. Help me not to enable but to have the wisdom to know when to get involved and when to distance myself.

Meditation Moments:

_____

_____

_____

_____

_____

_____

_____

_____

_____

_____

EMOTIONS

Emotion is often defined as a complex state of feeling that results in physical and psychological changes that influence thought and behavior. God created us to have emotions. There are positive emotions like happiness, excitement, love, joy, hope, contentment, relief, and calmness. There are negative emotions like anger, contempt, disgust, anxiety, embarrassment, fear, worry, doubt, envy, hurt, sadness, and boredom. How we process these emotions can have a physical and psychological effect on us. How we express our emotions to our children can be critical. Are the emotions I'm expressing of anger, fear, or hurt causing a deeper rift in the relationships I have with my children? Would expressing positive emotions help build a closer relationship with them? God created us to have emotions to protect us from harm and to enjoy him and all his creation. Satan would like to steal your joy by prompting you to focus on negative emotions and distorting our use of emotions.

Jesus is our example of the use of emotions. He was compassionate (Mark 6:34; NIV); full of joy (John 15:11; NIV); he wept (John 11:35; NIV); he was amazed (Matthew 8:10; NIV); he rejoiced (Luke 10:21; NIV); and he loved (John 11:5; NIV). He reflected God with his emotions.

Are the emotions you're experiencing positive or negative? Are they having a positive or negative effect on others around you? There will be legitimate times when you experience some negative emotions. We have to be careful that our negative emotions don't lead to sin. Let our emotions reflect a life that brings glory to God.

> (I Peter 5:7; NIV) "Cast all your anxiety on him because he cares for you."

> (John 15:11; NLT) "These things I have spoken to you so that my joy may be in you, and that your joy may be made full."

> (Proverbs 3:5-6; NIV) "Trust in the Lord with all your heart and do not lean on your own understanding. In all your ways submit to him, and he will make your paths straight."

(Isaiah 12:2; NIV) "Surely God is my salvation; I will trust and not be afraid. The Lord, the Lord himself is my strength and my defense; he has become my salvation."

Prayer: Lord, please help me to focus on you during times of trials and not my emotions. Help me experience those positive emotions that come from a vibrant relationship with you. Help me to discern when I'm focusing on negative emotions, and turn it around so that I get my focus back on you. Increase my faith so I can trust you more. Thank you for helping me to grow in this area so I can honor you and be a blessing to others.

Meditation Moments:

_____

_____

_____

_____

_____

_____

_____

_____

_____

_____

ENCOURAGEMENT

When we are wearied by life and the many challenges we face, we can become discouraged and lose sight of the One who really is in control. We try to control and craft our own solutions, which can be exhausting. In the book of (Psalms, 55:1-15; NLT), David cries out to God. He is so upset his heart is pounding. He is fearful and can't stop shaking. Then in verse 16, he says, "But, I will call on the Lord who rescues me." He acknowledged his problems and concerns to God, and then he says, "But I will..." He puts his trust in God. He recognizes that no matter what the problem is, he knows that God is there for him and that he cares for him. He determines to trust God. Our God cares for you, too.

Do you realize just how valued you and your children are in God's eyes? (Psalms 55:22; NLT) says, "Give your burdens to the Lord, and he will take care of you. He will not permit the godly to slip and fall." It says he will take care of you, not that he might, but that he will! In (Luke 12:6-7; NLT), Jesus shares with his followers, "What is the price of five sparrows—two copper coins? Yet God does not forget a single one of them. And the very hairs on your head are all numbered. So don't be afraid; you are more valuable to God than a whole flock of sparrows." You are so intimately known to God that even the hairs on your head are numbered.

(Jeremiah 1:5; NLT) says, "I knew you before I formed you in your mother's womb..." He is your Heavenly Father, who created you and loves you. God loves you and your children so very much. He wants what's best for you, just as you do for your children. He hears your prayers and sees your tears. (Ephesians 2:10; NIV) states, "For we are God's masterpiece. He has created us anew in Christ Jesus, so we can do the good things he planned for us long ago." You and your children are a masterpiece hand-created by God, however, we are all still works in process. Allow him the time to do his perfect work. Find encouragement in knowing, with all assurance, that you and your children are loved by God.

> (II Thessalonians. 2:16; NLT) "Now may our Lord Jesus Christ himself, and God our Father, who loved us and by his grace gave us eternal comfort and a wonderful hope, comfort you and strengthen you in every good thing you do and say."

(I Peter 1:4-6; NLT*)* "and we have a priceless inheritance—an inheritance that is kept in heaven for you, pure and undefiled, beyond the reach of change and decay. And through your faith, God is protecting you by his power until you receive this salvation, which is ready to be revealed on the last day for all to see. So be truly glad. There is wonderful joy ahead, even though you must endure many trials for a little while."

(Psalms 56:8; NLT*)* "You keep track of all my sorrows. You have collected all my tears in your bottle. You have recorded each one in your book."

(Proverbs 14:26; NIV*)* "Whoever fears the Lord has a secure fortress, and for their children it will be a refuge."

Prayer: Lord, how wonderful to know how much you love us and that you have a perfect plan for us. When I start to feel discouraged, remind me again of your great love for me and that you are working for my good and the good of my children. Thank you for your Word which brings me great encouragement. Thank you for the people you use to encourage me. Use me to encourage others.

Meditation Moments:

_____

_____

_____

_____

_____

_____

_____

_____

_____

EXAMPLES

The Bible is loaded with life examples that God uses to teach us. The book of Ruth is a great example of compassion and faithfulness. The book of Proverbs provides examples of how to live life wisely. Jesus was example of love, grace, and forgiveness. Let's look at the story in *John 8*. The religious leaders brought a woman to Jesus who had been caught in adultery. Their intent was to trap Jesus into saying something they could use against him.

They reminded him that the Law of Moses said to stone her. They asked Jesus what he had to say about that. Jesus didn't answer, but stooped down and wrote in the dust with his finger. Now look closely at what Jesus says to them in (John 8:7; NLT) "**7**They kept demanding an answer, so he stood up again and said, "All right, but let the one who has never sinned throw the first stone!" Wow, what a wise answer. They recognized they had all sinned at one time or another and they began walking away one by one. Then Jesus showed his amazing grace and forgiveness to the woman in (John 8:10-11; NLT) "**10**Then Jesus stood up again and said to the woman, "Where are your accusers? Didn't even one of them condemn you?" **11**"No, Lord," she said. And Jesus said, "Neither do I. Go and sin no more."

He forgave and then warned her to leave her life of sin. He didn't condemn or lecture her. What an example he showed of mercy, forgiveness, kindness, love, and patience.

In (John 13:15; NIV) Jesus says, "I have set you an example that you should do as I have done for you." Are we following Jesus' example? What kind of example are we being to others? Do our words reflect our actions? Can you think of people you have met during your life that were godly examples? Our Heavenly Father loves our children with a priceless, endless love. He created them, knows them, values them and loves them. Let us endeavor to follow Jesus' example and show love, mercy, forgiveness and patience to those around us.

(I Timothy 4:12; NIV) "Don't let anyone look down on you because you are young, but set an example for the believers in speech, in conduct, in love, in faith and in purity."

(Titus 2:7-8; NIV) "In everything set them an example by doing what is good. In your teaching show integrity, seriousness and soundness of speech that cannot be condemned, so that those who oppose you may be ashamed because they have nothing bad to say about us."

(Psalms 86:15; NIV) "But you, Lord, are a compassionate and gracious God, slow to anger, abounding in love and faithfulness."

Prayer: Lord, thank you for the many examples you have provided for us in your precious word. Help me to be a godly example to those around me, reflecting godly values and integrity. Help me to have the spiritual and physical disciplines necessary for a closer walk with you. Show me the changes I need to make in my life so that my example will attract others to you. To you be the glory forever.

Meditation Moments:

_____

_____

_____

_____

_____

_____

_____

_____

_____

_____

EXPECTATIONS

We all have certain expectations we live with: expectations about how we act toward others, and expectations about how we expect others to act. How do you handle it when others don't meet the expectations you have for them? Do you find yourself getting frustrated or impatient with people that don't meet your expectations? Do you think Jesus had expectations about his disciples? Jesus showed grace. He loved them, taught them, and trained them. In (Mark 10:33-34; NIV), while he was describing to his disciples the terrible death he would suffer, they were more concerned with who would sit closest to him in heaven. When Jesus was arrested, his closest followers all deserted him. Peter denied him three times after spending so much time with him. Yet, Jesus could see Peter's potential. In (Matthew 16:18; NIV), he called him the rock on which he would build his church.

When we look at others and they don't fall within the expectations we have about them, we often get judgmental and critical. The good news is that Jesus sees the heart of people and their future while we don't. Don't let your worldly expectations cause rifts in relationships when people don't measure up. We need to examine our hearts first. Have we met all of Jesus' expectations of where he feels we should be spiritually? Are we living up to our full potential as a Christ Follower serving God, his church and others? Aren't you glad Jesus sees our true worth and our potential? What wonderful news that we have such a patient, loving and understanding Father. Even with all our flaws, we are loved and valued by our Heavenly Father. He even calls us the apple of his eye. (Zechariah 2:8; NIV) states, "For this is what the Lord Almighty says: "After the Glorious One has sent me against the nations that have plundered you—for whoever touches you touches the apple of his eye."

> (Galatians 1:4; NIV) "who gave himself for our sins to rescue us from the present evil age, according to the will of our God and Father."

> (Galatians 5:6; NIV) "…the only thing that counts is faith expressing itself through love"

(Daniel 12:3; NLT) "Those who are wise will shine as bright as the sky, and those who lead many to righteousness will shine like the stars forever."

Prayer: Lord, thank you for reminding me to continue to fix my eyes on you. Help me during those times I am tempted to be critical or judgmental when others don't measure up to my expectations. Help me to see them instead through your loving eyes. If they are truly sinning and not just falling short of my expectations, then please give me the words to gently speak the truth in love. Then empower me to show them love, forgiveness and grace as you have repeatedly shown me.

Meditation Moments:

_____

_____

_____

_____

_____

_____

_____

_____

_____

FEAR

Fear is a distressing emotion aroused by real or imagined impending danger, evil, and pain. How do you cope when faced with fear? Do you run to God or away from God? Have you found yourself in situations that have filled you with fear, whether for yourself or your children? Danger, illness, change, bad news? Did you notice in the definition it says we can experience fear whether it's real or imagined? When we are going through something that causes fear, our enemy, Satan, wants to get us paralyzed by fear. God wants to use these times to grow our faith and trust in him. Where there is fear, there is no room for faith. (Isaiah 35:4; NLT) states, "Say to those with fearful hearts, 'Be strong, do not fear; your God will come, he will come with vengeance; with divine retribution, he will come to save you.'"

Fear is an important emotion that God provides for us in order to protect us from harm. However, he doesn't want us to live in a state of fear. (I John 4:18; NIV) states, "There is no fear in love. But perfect love drives out fear." No matter how bad the trial or the fear that is haunting you, God wants you to know he is still in control. In (Matthew 14:29-33; NLT), when Peter is walking toward Jesus on the water, it isn't until he takes his eyes off Jesus that he starts to sink. We can learn a lesson from that. If we take our eyes off Jesus and focus on our problems, then before we know it we are sinking into despair and fear.

Turn to Jesus and his Word and let his promises replace your fear with faith.

(Deuteronomy 31:8; NIV) "The Lord himself goes before you and will be with you; he will never leave you nor forsake you. Do not be afraid; do not be discouraged."

(Isaiah 41:13; NIV) "For I am the Lord your God, who takes hold of your right hand and says to you, do not fear; I will help you."

(Psalms 34:9; NIV) "Fear the Lord, you his holy people, for those who fear him lack nothing."

(Psalms 56:3; NIV) "When I am afraid, I put my trust in you."

Prayer: Lord we want to trust you more. We know that you are the creator of all things and you are in control. Replace our fears with your perfect peace. Give us wisdom so we know how to handle this situation in accordance with your perfect will. We will proclaim your promises. We will put our trust in you, confident that you know what is best. All praise and glory to God our Father.

Meditation Moments:

_____

_____

_____

_____

_____

_____

_____

_____

_____

FINDING JOY

I admire how Paul maintains his joy while in the worst of circumstances. He suffered beatings, hunger, thirst, imprisonment, and shipwreck for proclaiming his faith in God (II Corinthians 11:23-27; NLT). He wrote several books in the New Testament while in jail, yet his writings were not looking for sympathy. He wrote encouraging words to the church and prayed they would be filled with joy. Read (Philippians 1:4; NLT) "In all my prayers for all of you, I always pray with joy." How does your lack of joy reflect to others? Do they see you with a sad, sour face or is joy emanating from within? Would your children describe you as joyful and full of peace? Would you rather be around unhappy people or joyful people? I know I would rather surround myself with people who have joy. Just being around them makes me smile.

Some people believe if they had more money, better job, better relationships, they would be happy and joyful. Joy doesn't come from our circumstances, but from peace within our heart. God's Holy Spirit is within those who believe in Christ and ask him into their hearts. That empowering of the Holy Spirit is what gives us inner joy despite our circumstances. If you haven't asked Christ into your heart, there is a prayer at the end of this book that I encourage you to read so that you too can have peace and find true joy.

Going through trials is never easy. Like the apostle Paul, we can find joy in the midst of the trial. How did he do that? He got his strength from God. In (Philippians 4:12-13; NIV), he wrote, "I know what it is to be in need, and I know what it is to have plenty. I have learned the secret of being content in any and every situation, whether well fed or hungry, whether living in plenty or in want. I can do all this through him who gives me strength."

We can rely on God and call on him to give us strength to get through trials. In (Psalms 59:17: NIV), David says, "You are my strength, I sing praise to you; you, God, are my fortress, my God on whom I can rely." David recognized he couldn't rely on himself. If we go through life on our own strength, we'll be disappointed. Let your strength come from God as you trust him more. God can give you peace and joy during the storms. Let the joy you receive as you grow in your personal relationship with Jesus shine as a light to those around you. As you find your joy again, let it be contagious.

(Psalms 16:11; NIV) "You make known to me the path of life; you will fill me with joy in your presence, with eternal pleasures at your right hand."

(Colossians 1:11-12; NIV) "being strengthened with all power according to his glorious might so that you may have great endurance and patience, and giving joyful thanks to the Father, who has qualified you to share in the inheritance of his holy people in the kingdom of light.

(John 17:13; NIV) "I am coming to you now, but I say these things while I am still in the world, so that they may have the full measure of my joy within them."

(Psalms 97:11; NLT) "Light shines on the godly, and joy for those whose hearts are right."

Prayer: Lord, thank you for giving me peace and joy. No matter the situation, you are here with me. You are in control. You can give me the strength we need. I can be joyful because my trust is in you. Continue to fill me with your joy. May the joy you provide me overflow and bring joy to others.

Meditation Moments:

_____

_____

_____

_____

_____

_____

_____

_____

FINDING REST

Rush, rush, rush…from the minute we crawl out of bed until we crash into it at night. Does that sound like you? Never enough time to get all the things done you had planned? I'm here to tell you it is okay to find those moments when you can just REST. No matter who you are, whether single mom, faithful volunteer, or CEO, God has commanded that we make time to rest. In *Exodus*, God told Moses that on the seventh day they were to make it a day of rest (Exodus 34:21: NLT). We need to find the time to quiet our bodies and minds which puts us in the best place to be able to hear from God and be used by God. What happens when we get too busy? Do we become so physically and emotionally drained that we have nothing left for our loved ones?

Time is one of our most important commodities. In (II Corinthians 5:10; NLT) and (Romans 14:12; NLT), God says we will give an account of how we spent our lives. God is more than able to help you accomplish what is important. Consider where your time is spent each day. Identify those time wasters like TV, internet, computer games, and social media. While they may be entertaining, are they the best way for you to spend your time? Can that time be better spent calling your kids and telling them you are thinking of them and love them? Can you think of ways you can make time in your schedule to rest in God's presence together? Maybe take them out for a meal or coffee for some one on one time to give them an opportunity to just rest from their busy schedules. Ask God to help you use your time wisely and to help yo0u have quality time in your family relationships. Take a deep breath, close your eyes, and find your rest in God.

> (Matthew 11:28; NLT) "Then Jesus said, "Come to me, all you who are weary and carry heavy burdens, and I will give you rest."

> (Psalms 62:5; NIV) "Yes, my soul, find rest in God; my hope comes from him."

> (Psalms 37:7; NIV) "Be still before the Lord and wait patiently for him; do not fret when people succeed in their ways, when they carry out their wicked schemes."

(Psalms 127:2; NIV) "In vain you rise early and stay up late, toiling for food to eat— for he grants sleep to those he loves."

Prayer: Lord, thank you for reminding me that I need to rest. Help me to use my time wisely and bring honor to you. Help me to make quality time with my family. I pray you will help them to find time to rest from their busy schedules. Thank you for knowing what we need and making a way for us to find rest.

Meditation Moments:

_____

_____

_____

_____

_____

_____

_____

_____

_____

_____

FORGIVENESS

"You are forgiven!" What beautiful words they are to the condemned, our guilt and shame washed away by Jesus when we give our hearts to him. (Acts 10:43; NIV) states, "All the prophets testify about him that everyone who believes in him receives forgiveness of sins through his name." Jesus freely gave all to bring us forgiveness while we were still sinners. (Romans 3:23; NIV) "For all have sinned and fall short of the glory of God." God freely forgave us and we are to strive to be like Christ. (I John 2:6; NIV) "whoever claims to live in him, must live as Jesus did." When someone we love offends us or sins against us are we quick to forgive or to condemn? "How many times should we forgive someone, seven times?" the disciples asked Jesus. Jesus replied, "I tell you, not seven times, but 77 times." In other words, keep forgiving. However, keep in mind that you need to exercise common sense as well. You are to forgive, but still exercise wisdom and set up parameters or boundaries to protect yourself from harmful situations when necessary.

Unforgiveness can block communication with God. (Mark 11:25; NIV) says, "And when you stand praying, if you hold anything against anyone, forgive them so that your father in Heaven may forgive you of your sins." Another danger of hanging on to unforgiveness is that it can create a bitterness inside. When that bitterness festers, it can lead to depression. (Hebrews 12:15: NIV) "See to it that no one falls short of the grace of God and that no bitter root grows up to cause trouble and defile many." How many people would feel better within their hearts, if they would learn to forgive others? Forgiveness is as freeing for you as it is to the other person.

> (Luke 11:4; NIV) "Forgive us our sins, for we also forgive everyone who sins against us. And lead us not into temptation"

> (II Corinthians 2:7; NIV) "Now instead, you ought to forgive and comfort him, so that he will not be overwhelmed by excessive sorrow."

> (Acts 13:38; NIV) "Therefore, my friends, I want you to know that through Jesus the forgiveness of sins is proclaimed to you."

(Psalms 86:5; NIV) "You, Lord, are forgiving and good, abounding in love to all who call to you."

(Lamentations 3:22-23; NIV) "Because of the Lord's great love we are not consumed, for his compassions never fail. They are new every morning; great is your faithfulness."

Prayer: Lord, thank you for your forgiveness. Search my heart and reveal any unforgiveness I'm hanging on to. I repent of all unforgiveness and ask that you would bring healing to me and to anyone I've been harboring unforgiveness toward. I know that it is your desire that we forgive others as you have so generously forgiven us. Give me wisdom in those relationships. I receive your forgiveness and I forgive them. Thank you for the healing work you do in both our lives.

Meditation Moments:

_____

_____

_____

_____

_____

_____

_____

_____

GRACE

Think back to where you were and what was going on in your life when you finally realized your need for a personal relationship with God. Where you living a selfish, self-centered life? Did you have sin in your life? It's easy to see sin in others and not ourselves. (Matthew 7:3; NLT) "Why do you look at the speck of sawdust in your brother's eye and pay not attention to the plank in your own eye?" What does God show us daily? Grace. His amazing grace is why we are saved. We are not saved for our good deeds, but by the grace of God and faith in his son, Jesus.

We're quick to judge others who aren't at the same spiritual level that we are at. (Matthew 7:1; NLT) "Do not judge others and you will not be judged." I know, I've been guilty of that myself. I pleaded with God, "Why can't they see that what they are doing is wrong?"

What we can learn is that our timing is not God's timing. God is still at work in our children's lives even when we can't see it. Who loves your children more than you? God does! He desires that all are to be saved. Ask God to show you how to love them where they are at. We don't have to approve of the sin, but we can love the sinner. This is not easy, but the rewards are great.

We need to exercise our faith in God. (Hebrews 11:1: NIV) "Now faith is confidence in what we hope for and assurance about what we do not see." In Ezekiel chapter 37, the writer tells how God turned a valley of dead bones back to life. Don't limit the power of God in our children's lives.

Be encouraged. We serve a mighty God and nothing is impossible for him. (Matthew 19:26; NIV) "Jesus looked at them and said, 'With man this is impossible, but with God all things are possible.'"

In (Romans 8:34: NIV) we are told, "Who then is the one who condemns? No one. Christ Jesus who died—more than that, who was raised to life—is at the right hand of God and is also interceding for us." Isn't it wonderful to know that our Lord Jesus is interceding for us and for our children.

> (Isaiah 59:21; NLT) "And this is my covenant with them," says the Lord. "My Spirit will not leave them, and neither will these words I have given you. They will be on your lips and on the lips of your children and your children's children forever. I, the Lord, have spoken!"

(Deuteronomy 5:29; NIV) "Oh, that their hearts would be inclined to fear me and keep all my commands always, so that it might go well with them and their children forever!"

(Psalms 128:6; NLT) "May you live to enjoy your grandchildren. May Israel have peace!"

(Isaiah 49:25: NLT) "But the Lord says, "The captives of warriors will be released, and the plunder of tyrants will be retrieved. For I will fight those who fight you, and I will save your children."

Prayer: Lord, I am so thankful that you love my children so much. Thank you for the work you are doing in their lives to help them know you more. Thank you for the grace you shower on us daily. Show me what I can do to show them love even though I don't approve of their lifestyle. I will patiently wait for you to bring them to a full knowledge of your love and salvation.

Meditation Moments:

_____

_____

_____

_____

_____

_____

_____

_____

_____

_____

GUIDANCE

Like the railings on the sides of a bridge or narrow road, God's word is the guard rail that protects us and shows us how to live life right. How else does God guide us? Through the guidance of his Holy Spirit. (Mark 1:8; NIV) states, "I baptize you with water, but he will baptize you with the Holy Spirit." He not only gives us his Holy Spirit, he also empowers us. In (Luke 24:49; NLT), Jesus told his disciples they will receive power when the Holy Spirit comes upon them. That power, along with daily learning God's Word, will guide you in life. Also, God will often put people around you that you can consult. It's helpful to seek the counsel of a trusted church leader or counselor.

Ever feel like you or one of your family has fallen off track? Don't despair. There is always hope with God. First make sure you are on track by daily spending time in God's Word and prayer. Next, let's ask God for a new infilling of his Holy Spirit so we can be empowered to be a guiding light to others. As we live a lifestyle of obedience to God, and daily seek his guidance for our own lives, others will see the changes in our life and God will be glorified. May his Spirit living in us shine like a beacon to those who have lost their way.

> (Psalms 16:7; NIV) "I will praise the Lord, who counsels me. Even at night my heart instructs me."

> (Isaiah 57:15; NIV) "For this is what the high and exalted One says—he who lives forever, whose name is holy: 'I live in a high and holy place, but also with the one who is contrite and lowly in spirit, to revive the spirit of the lowly and to revive the heart of the contrite.'"

> (Proverbs 11:14; NIV) "For lack of guidance a nation falls, but victory is won through many advisers."

> (Hebrews 5:2; NIV) "He is able to deal gently with those who are ignorant and are going astray, since he himself is subject to weakness."

(Philippians 2:15; NIV) "So that you may become blameless and pure, children of God without fault in a warped and crooked generation. Then you will shine among them like stars in the sky."

Prayer: Lord, I thank you for guiding me. Continue to guide my family and me according to your perfect plan for us. I pray for a fresh renewal of your Holy Spirit. Help me to continue to study your word daily. Use me to be a light to those around me that points others to you. I pray for my children to be led by your spirit in their lives. Guide our family to paths that lead to strong spiritual disciplines. Guide us by your perfect love.

Meditation Moments:

_____

_____

_____

_____

_____

_____

_____

GUILT

Guilt comes with baggage like shame, regret, and embarrassment, just to name a few. We have all done things we had guilt over. Our children are probably carrying around their own burdens of guilt and shame. You have already beaten yourself up over the "could haves, should haves, and what ifs." God doesn't want us walking around with guilt and condemnation. He conquered those on Calvary. He came to give us a new life and life style. (John 10:10; NIV) "The thief comes only to steal, kill, and destroy. I have come that they may have life, and have it to the full." We may be imperfect people but we have a perfect Heavenly Father who loves us with an everlasting love.

After King David sinned with Bathsheba, he acknowledged his sin to God. (Psalms 51:4: NIV) "Against you, you only, have I sinned and done what is evil in your sight; so you are right in your verdict and justified when you judge."

Good news: Jesus wants to forgive us AND we need to forgive ourselves and our children. Are you harboring guilt over things said or done in your relationship with your children? Let God's love pour over you to cleanse you from all guilt and shame. Let go of any guilt you are hanging on to. Pray for your children that may be carrying around their own heavy burden of guilt in their lives. (Philippians 3:13-15; NIV) states, "Brothers and sisters, I do not consider myself yet to have taken hold of it. But one thing I do: Forgetting what is behind and straining toward what is ahead, I press on toward the goal to win the prize for which God has called me heavenward in Christ Jesus." All of us, then, who are mature, should take such a view of things. And if on some point you think differently, that too God will make clear to you. Once you've asked God to forgive you and you've forgiven yourself, ask God to show you what your next step is to build up the relationships in your family.

> (1 John 1:7; NIV) "But if we walk in the light, as he is in the light, we have fellowship with one another, and the blood of Jesus, his Son, purifies us from all sin."

> (Romans 8:1-2; NIV) "Therefore, there is now no condemnation for those who are in Christ Jesus,"

(Psalms 32:5; NIV) "Then I acknowledged my sin to you and did not cover up my iniquity. I said, 'I will confess my transgressions to the Lord.' And you forgave the guilt of my sin."

Prayer: Lord, I realize I've done many things in my past that have caused me guilt and shame. I repent of them right now. I know you came to forgive me and cleanse me of all sin. I receive your forgiveness and I forgive myself. I let go of condemning thoughts and receive your healing for my mind and soul. I pray for my children that are carrying around guilt and shame. Direct their paths to you. I pray they may find forgiveness, healing and peace for their lives. Show me what my next steps are to show more love and to build up my family relationships. Thank you Lord for taking away our guilt and giving us hope.

Meditation Moments:

_____

_____

_____

_____

_____

_____

_____

_____

_____

HOPE

Do you feel like you've lost hope? Are your children going through situations where they feel hopeless? Where can we turn when our hope has dwindled and we're discouraged? Let me give you four steps to help restore your hope.

First, we turn to Jesus Christ and tell him our cares and concerns. Turn to him and ask him to help you through this trial. He created you and loves you and your family with an undying love. He wants to help you. Many of us have that prideful attitude of "I can fix this myself," or "I don't need help," impatiently acting, when we should be waiting on God. It's not our place to try to fix everything. What if, by doing things 'your way', you hinder God from doing things 'his' way? Put your hope into God and his almighty abilities and not into your own meager efforts.

Second, turn to the many promises he has given us in his word. I can't emphasize enough how important it is to take time to read God's Word every day. Are you fearful, angry, hurt, or sad? Look up verses on those topics for whatever you are going through and see what God says about it. (Psalms 119:105; NLT) says, "Your word is a lamp to guide my feet and a light for my path." Let his word guide you on the right path.

Third, connect with other Christians. God doesn't want us doing life alone. We are all part of God's family. We are here to help, encourage, pray with and love one another. Many of us were taught to be self-sufficient, which is a good thing, but not when we are trying to do things that only God can do. (Matthew 18:20; NLT) states, "For where two or three gather together as my followers, I am there among them." Find encouragement and strength by being with other Christians. Seek out Christian counselors if you still need additional help.

Fourth, place your trust in God. God is not ignoring you. He hears you. He heard the very first prayer you made. He loves you. He wants you to turn to him. Trust he is in control even when it's difficult. We are reminded that we walk by faith, not sight.

> (II Corinthians 4:18; NLT) says, "So we don't look at the troubles we can see now; rather, we fix our gaze on things that cannot be seen. For the things we see now will soon be gone, but the things we cannot see will last forever."

Rejoice! Know that God hears you and will answer your prayers. (Romans 12:12; NLT) reads, "Rejoice in our confident hope. Be patient in trouble, and keep on praying." It doesn't say to rejoice only when our prayers are answered. You can rejoice and be hopeful because you have the confidence in knowing God has heard your prayers and have hope he will do what is best.

> (Isaiah 65:23; NIV) "They will not labor in vain, nor will they bear children doomed to misfortune; for they will be a people blessed by the Lord, they and their descendants with them."

> (Philippians 4:6; NIV) "Do not be anxious about anything, but in every situation, by prayer and petition, with thanksgiving, present your requests to God."

> (Psalms 31:24; NLT) "So be strong and courageous, all you who put your hope in the Lord!"

> (Psalms 42:11; NIV) "Why, my soul, are you downcast? Why so disturbed within me? Put your hope in God, for I will yet praise him, my Savior and my God."

Prayer: Lord, you know that I've had times of discouragement and loss of hope. I now choose to put my hope in you and not in myself or others. You will never fail me or leave me. Help me to redirect those negative thoughts to focus on your promises. Lift my children from feelings of hopelessness. Help them see your hand moving in their lives. Restore their hope in you. Help me to share hope and encouragement with them. I know you have a plan for my life and for my family. I accept where you have me right now. Help me to be patient while I wait for you to answer my prayers.

Meditation Moments:

_____

_____

_____

_____

_____

_____

_____

_____

_____

HURTS

It may not be like physical pain, but emotional pain can hurt. Broken hearts and broken relationships can be very painful. In the Bible, there are many accounts of broken people crying out to a compassionate God. In many of the Psalms, David cried out in anguish to God. In (Psalms 42:3; NIV) he cries, "My tears have been my food day and night, while men say to me all day long, 'Where is your God?'" Where is God when we are in pain from hurts caused by those we love? He is holding you up and carrying you in his loving, tender arms. Find your rest in his presence. Get alone with God and as you pour your heart to him, listen for his quiet voice. He will bring comfort and healing. Read out loud God's promises. Recall all the things he has done for you in the past. He was there with you in the past and he is here with you in the present. He will see you through this season. He is the God who heals. He can restore those broken relationships and make them new.

We read in (Isaiah 29:24; NIV), "Those who are wayward in spirit will gain understanding; those who complain will accept instruction." He can change our stubborn, prideful, hurting hearts and he can change our children's hearts as well. (Romans 5:6; NIV) states, "You see, at just the right time, when we were still powerless, Christ died for the ungodly." Christ gave his life for all, even the ungodly and unholy. God's restoration power alone can wash away the pain and the hurt of our broken hearts and replace it with peace and joy.

(Psalms 120:1; NIV) "I call on the Lord in my distress, and he answers me."

(Psalms 138:3; NLT) "As soon as I pray, you answer me; you encourage me by giving me strength."

(Psalms 18:6; NLT) "But in my distress, I cried out to the Lord; yes, I prayed to my God for help. He heard me from his sanctuary; my cry to him reached his ears."

(II Chronicles 33:12; NIV) "In his distress he sought the favor of the Lord his God and humbled himself greatly before the God of his ancestors."

Prayer: Lord, you see my broken heart, my tears, my anguish and despair. Bring healing and restoration to these broken relationships. I know you won't fail me. Help me to see your hand working in this situation. Thank you for never failing me. Your ways are always perfect. Thank you for comforting me and carrying me through this season.

Meditation Moments:

_____

_____

_____

_____

_____

_____

_____

_____

_____

JUDGING

Jesus: accused, yet innocent of sin. Judged as guilty, then condemned to death by hanging on the cross. Jesus died for our sins. (Romans 5:8; NIV) "But God demonstrates his own love for us in this: while we were still sinners, Christ died for us." We are born with a sinful nature, yet he gave his life for us when we didn't deserve it. While he was dying on the cross, Jesus said in (Luke 23:34; NLT), "Jesus said, "Father, forgive them for they don't know not what they are doing. And they divided up his clothes by casting lots."

The Bible says we have no excuse when we pass judgment on others. We show contempt for God's kindness, tolerance, and patience. Hasn't God been kind, tolerant and patient many times in our lives? Isn't that person we are judging also able to receive God's kindness, patience and mercy as well?

How do we handle the situations where sin is prevalent and poor behavior and bad choices continue? We can easily judge others as lazy, selfish, self-centered, and that judgment could be true, but it's a fine line between observing and judging. God can see our hearts and motives. Our God, who is rich in mercy, withheld judgement for us while we were sinners, when he could have easily come down and wiped us out.

An effective way to avoiding judging others is to ask God to give you a discerning spirit so you can judge wisely. (Hebrews 4:13; NIV) states, "Nothing in all creation is hidden from God's sight. Everything is uncovered and laid bare before the eyes of him to whom we must give an account." Seek to encourage our loved ones instead of criticizing and being judgmental. Ask God to fill you with a loving heart and take away any critical spirit.

Then your light will shine in the darkness.

> (Matthew 5:16; NIV) "In the same way, let your light shine before others, that they may see your good deeds and glorify your Father in heaven."

> (Romans 2:1-3; NIV) "You, therefore, have no excuse, you who pass judgement on someone else, for at whatever point you judge the other, you are condemning yourself, because you who pass judgment do the same things."

(John 7:24; NIV) "Stop judging by mere appearances, but instead judge correctly."

(Psalms 41:1; NIV) "Blessed are those who have regard for the weak; the Lord delivers them in times of trouble."

Prayer: Lord, thank you for your tolerance and patience with me as you help me daily to be more like you. Take away any critical and bitter nature and replace it with a discerning heart so I can make wise judgements. Fill me with a loving, kind spirit. Help me to encourage others instead of judging.

Meditation Moments:

KINDNESS

Jesus was pretty clear in (Luke 6:35-36; NIV) when he gave instructions on kindness. It reads, "But love your enemies, do good to them and lend to them without expecting to get anything back. Then your reward will be great and you will be children of the most-high, because he is kind to the ungrateful and wicked."

Have you ever been so frustrated with others that you had unkind words to say? Sometimes we can be unkind to those closest to us, kids and spouses. We sometimes take them for granted. If God is telling us to be kind to the ungrateful and wicked, shouldn't we be kind to those closest to us, to those imperfect children, loved by imperfect parents? Ask God to help you be strong enough and courageous enough to let God write their story. Christian speaker Lisa Turnquist said, "When you speak to your children, speak to their potential, not their mistakes."

Follow God's example of loving the ungrateful, as he has shown love and kindness to us during our times of being ungrateful and unappreciative of all our Heavenly Father has done for us.

What are some random acts of kindness you can do for your family today? Do it without an agenda or expecting to be reciprocated, purely to show kindness. Let it generate a new spark of joy and healing in your relationships.

> (I Corinthians 13:4; NIV) "Love is patient, love is kind. It does not envy, it does not boast, it is not proud."

> (Ephesians 4:32; NIV) "Be kind and compassionate to one another, forgiving each other, just as Christ God forgave you."

> (I Thessalonians 5:15; NIV) "Make sure that nobody pays back wrong for wrong, but always strive to do what is good for each other and for everyone else."

> (Micah 6:8; NIV) "He has shown all you, O mortal, what is good. And what does the Lord require of you? To act justly and to love mercy and to walk humbly with your God."

(Titus 3:4-5; NIV) "But when the kindness and love of God our Savior appeared, He saved us, not because of righteous things we had done, but because of his mercy. He saved us through the washing of rebirth and renewal by the Holy Spirit."

Prayer: Lord, forgive me if I've been unkind to anyone. You have shown amazing kindness to me although I wasn't worthy. Help me to be more like you, showing kindness to the ungrateful and unappreciative. Help me to see others through your eyes, to see past the outside and past the behavior. I'm so thankful for your great kindness to me and my family. Thank you for blessing us.

Meditation Moments:

_____

_____

_____

_____

_____

_____

_____

_____

_____

LETTING GO

We watched as some of our loved ones were going through a time of making poor choices. They were in denial of their problem and the destruction it was causing those around them. I tried reasoning with them but they weren't listening. I wanted to fix it, and run over and talk some sense into them, try to make them see the error of their ways. I wanted to help them, but didn't know what else to do. Then my sweet husband gave me a word of wisdom to 'Let Go and Let God' handle it. He could see that I was so consumed with thoughts of the problems that it was eating me up. He was right. It was time for me to put my faith in God. (Matthew 21:22; NIV) states, "If you believe, you will receive whatever you ask for in prayer." As I prayed I began feeling impressed by the Holy Spirit to hold back and not do or say anything for now. Although it took strength, I held myself back and kept quiet. Then I would remind myself of God's promises: He can do all things; he can do more than I can even imagine; nothing is impossible with God; God knows exactly what to do. Though I was sick to my stomach with turmoil inside, I continued to repeat God's many promises. I told God, "This is really hard, but I put them into your hands." I came across a great scripture in (Isaiah 29:17; NIV) that says, "The wayward in spirit will gain understanding; those who complain will accept instruction." That gave me hope. I completely released myself and them into God's care.

What I found a short time later was that I had a great peace inside. (Psalms 94:19; NLT) reads, "When doubts filled my mind, your comfort gave me renewed hope and cheer." I had obeyed God by trusting him instead to trying to fix things on my own. As the days unfolded, I stayed away and continued to pray, put my trust in God and asked some strong Christians to pray with me. God worked miracles and things happened that only God could have done. He is faithful to his word. God can bring you a greater peace than you have ever known as you learn to let go and trust him.

(II Corinthians 5:7; NIV) "For we live by faith, not by sight."

(John 14:1; NLT) "Do not let your hearts be troubled. Trust in God; trust also in me."

(Psalms 94:12-13; NIV) "Blessed is the one you discipline, Lord, the one you teach from your law; you grant them relief from days of trouble, till a pit is dug for the wicked."

(Psalms 112:7; NIV) *"They* will have no fear of bad news; their hearts are steadfast, trusting in the Lord."

Prayer: Lord, I commit my family to your tender loving care. I love them so much, yet you love them so much more. Help me to trust you more with my children. Help me to have the wisdom to know when it is time to Let Go and Let God. I will put my trust in you. When I'm missing peace and feeling anxious, show me what I need to change in my attitude or behavior that may be stopping my peace. Show me when I am relying on myself and not you. Show me if I am speaking negative words instead of remembering your promises. Thank you for being such a loving, understanding God and Father.

Meditation Moments:

_____

_____

_____

_____

_____

_____

_____

_____

LISTENING

Every day we are faced with choices from the moment we awake, like what clothes will we wear, what food to eat, and where will we go today. God has given us the freedom to choose. One important choice we make is listening. While it may seem like something we do automatically, we are choosing to what we listen. We might choose to listen to the radio while driving instead of listening to the kids whining from the back seat for the tenth time, "Are we there yet?" Okay, I have to agree, I'd probably choose the radio too at that point. However, there are times when it is very important to choose to be a good listener. It also isn't very easy. We must choose to actively quiet our minds to clearly hear what the other person is saying. (Proverbs 15:31; NLT) states, "If you listen to constructive criticism, you are at home among the wise." Sometimes pride gets in the way of good listening. We can get more concerned with what we are saying or are going to say, than to listen carefully to what the other person has to say. In other words, we feel that what we have to say is more important than what they have to say. Sounds like pride, doesn't it?

Listening is important in our relationships, but also in our spiritual walk. How well are we listening to God speak to us? In I Kings 19; NIV) the Lord spoke to Elijah with a gentle whisper. Have you heard those quiet whispers from the Lord? Isaiah 30:21; NIV) says, "Whether you turn to the right or to the left, your ears will hear a voice behind you, saying, 'This is the way; walk in it.'"

(I John 5:14-15; NIV) states, "This is the confidence we have in approaching God: that if we ask anything according to his will, he hears us. And if we know that he hears us—whatever we ask—we know that we have what we asked of him." Aren't you glad to know that our God hears us when we talk to him? (John 10:27; NIV) states, "My sheep listen to my voice; I know them, and they follow me." Ask the Lord to show you how to be a better listener. It will improve your relationships because it will show others that what they have to say is important.

> (John 5:24; NIV) "Very truly I tell you, whoever hears my word and believes him who sent me has eternal life and will not be judged but has crossed over from death to life."

(Revelation 3:20; NIV) "Here I am! I stand at the door and knock. If anyone hears my voice and opens the door, I will come in and eat with that person, and they with me."

(John 8:47; NIV) Anyone who belongs to God listens gladly to the words of God..."

(Romans 10:17; NIV) "Consequently, faith comes from hearing the message, and the message is heard through the word about Christ."

Prayer: Lord, help me to clearly hear you. Thank you for hearing me when I pray to you. Thank you for being so faithful to your word. Help me to listen more sincerely when others are talking to me. Show me those times when I'm distracted and not listening well, so I can improve. I want to bring you honor in this area of my life. I'm so grateful you hear me.

Meditation Moments:

_____

_____

_____

_____

_____

_____

_____

_____

_____

_____

LOSS OF A CHILD

Loss can be devastating to a family. As parents who lost a child to an accident, we understand how crippling pain and grief can be. That grief can affect each family member differently in how they cope. Some get angry, some try to bury it, some self-medicate with drugs or alcohol, some blame God or turn away from God. Loss is the best time to turn towards God. No one knows when or how we will die. That is why it is so important to know where our eternal home will be.

He is our great comforter. (Isaiah 49:13; NIV) reads, "Shout for joy, you heavens; rejoice, you earth; burst into song, you mountains! For the Lord comforts his people and will have compassion on his afflicted ones." We may never find the answers to why God allowed a bad thing to happen till we get to Heaven, but we can be assured he is with us during those difficult times. In the book of Daniel, King Nebuchadnezzar had Shadrach, Meshach and Abednego bound and thrown into the blazing furnace for their faith in God. The King was shocked to see a fourth person in the furnace with them. (Daniel 3:25; NIV) reads," He (King Nebuchadnezzar) said, 'Look! I see four men walking around in the fire, unbound and unharmed, and the fourth looks like a son of the gods.'" Be assured, God is walking with you as you walk through the fiery storm of loss.

For those in your family suffering loss, let me encourage you to love on them and show them grace, patience and kindness. Let them know you are there for them to listen when they need someone to talk to or a shoulder to cry on. Invite them to attend a grief support program like GriefShare. If you are grieving the loss of a child, remember God can heal broken hearts. The enemy wants to fill your mind with all the 'what ifs' or 'if onlys', but God wants to fill you with his peace. (John 14:27; NIV) reads, "Peace I leave with you; my peace I give you. I do not give to you as the world gives. Do not let your hearts be troubled and do not be afraid." Receive his peace and let him comfort your broken heart.

> (II Corinthians 1:3-4; NIV) "Praise be to the God and Father of our Lord Jesus Christ, the Father of compassion and the God of all comfort, who comforts us in all our troubles, so that we can comfort those in any trouble with the comfort we ourselves receive from God."

(Jeremiah 31:13; NIV) "Then young women will dance and be glad, young men and old as well. I will turn their mourning into gladness; I will give them comfort and joy instead of sorrow."

(Isaiah 61:2; NIV) "...to proclaim the year of the Lord's favor and the day of vengeance of our God, to comfort all who mourn."

(Matthew 5:4; NIV) "Blessed are those who mourn, for they will be comforted."

Prayer: Lord, you see when our hearts are broken and every tear that falls. We pray you will fill us with your comfort and peace. We are hurting but we will hold on to your promises to carry us through. Lead us to godly people and resources that will help us during this time. In you alone we find true peace and comfort.

Meditation Moments:

_____

_____

_____

_____

_____

_____

_____

_____

PATIENCE

The definition of patience is the power or capacity to endure something difficult or disagreeable without complaint. It's easy to fall short in this area in this age of instant gratification. We want our prayers answered NOW. I'm thankful that God was patient with me and didn't answer some of my prayers immediately, as that would not have been what was best for me. Just because we can't always see God moving in our family's lives doesn't mean he is not at work. He gives us patience to endure in difficult times. (Colossians 1: 11;NIV) "...being strengthened with all power according to his glorious might so that you may have great endurance and patience."

I get it, waiting is hard, but the benefits are worth it. It is far better to wait on God's timing than to try to direct a situation from our worldly perspective. Have you ever experienced a time when you were just about to give up on something you prayed about, and then God came through with an an answered prayer? They say God answers prayer with a Yes, No or Wait. Wait does not mean a No. God may have a perfectly good reason why you haven't received a certain answer to prayer. Perhaps the timing isn't right. Whatever the delay, we should praise God that he knows what is best and his timing is always perfect. (Romans 15:5; NLT) states, "May the God who gives endurance and encouragement give you the same attitude of mind toward each other that Christ Jesus had." Reading the Bible, the inspired Word of God, gives us hope and encouragement as we wait patiently for God's promises to be fulfilled. God will empower you to endure trials and to patiently wait for his answers to your prayers.

> (Colossians 3:12; NIV) "Therefore, as God's chosen people, holy and dearly loved, clothe yourselves with compassion, kindness, humility, gentleness and patience."

> (James 5:8; NIV) "You too, be patient and stand firm, because the Lord's coming is near."

> (Psalms 40:1; NIV) "I waited patiently for the Lord; he turned to me and heard my cry."

(Ephesians 4:2; NIV) "Be completely humble and gentle; be patient, bearing with one another in love."

(Ecclesiastes 8:6; NIV) "For there is a proper time and procedure for every matter, though a person may be weighed down by misery."

Prayer: Lord, thank you for being so patient with me. Please help me to exercise more patience. I desire to be more like you. You are full of love, kindness and patience toward your people. Replace my impatience with your peace and wisdom to deal with the situation that's making me impatient.

Meditation Moments:

_____

_____

_____

_____

_____

_____

_____

_____

_____

PEACE

Are you experiencing peace right now, or struggling with chaos? Is there a part of your life in which you would like to have more peace, like at work, in relationships, or even with yourself? You can seek God to ask him to show you how to bring peace to the current situation. Let's examine what the Bible tells us about peace, and find out how we can bring peace to the chaos around us. (Psalms 34:14; NLT) says we are to search for peace and work to maintain it. (Ephesians 6:15; NLT) also says we are to put on peace. (Philippians 4:7; NIV) says we experience God's peace.

Determine not to speak a negative word to that person that you're not a peace with. (Mark 9:50; NIV) says, "...be at peace with each other." Show complete love, grace, kindness and patience even though it may not be reciprocated. Perhaps send a peace offering with no strings attached with word or gifts from a heart of sincere love, then leave the rest to God. God is our healer and restorer. Stay strong in reading God's word, as (Isaiah 26:3; NLT) states, "You will keep in perfect peace all who trust in you, all whose thoughts are fixed on you." (Isaiah 9:6; NLT) states, "...And he will be called Wonderful Counselor, Mighty God, Everlasting Father, Prince of Peace." Jesus said in (John 16:33; NLT), "I have told you all this so that you may have peace in me. Here on earth you will have many trials and sorrows. But take heart because I have overcome the world."

So, take heart my dear friends, and find peace from God, the peace that passes all understanding.

> (Ephesians 2:14; NIV) "For he himself is our peace, who has made the two groups one and has destroyed the barrier, the dividing wall of hostility."

> (I Thessalonians 5:23; NIV) "May God himself, the God of peace, sanctify you through and through. May your whole spirit, soul and body be kept blameless at the coming of our Lord Jesus Christ."

> (Isaiah 26:12; NLT) "Lord, you will grant us peace; all we have accomplished is really from you."

(Matthew 5:9; NLT) "God blesses those who work for peace, for they will be called the children of God."

Prayer: Lord, thank you for being a God of peace and for your promises of peace through your word. Show me what I can do to bring peace to my life and those around me. Bring healing and restore any broken relationships in my life. Thank you so much for the work you are doing in my live and in my loved ones lives. Thank you for bringing us your perfect peace that passes all understanding.

Meditation Moments:

_____

_____

_____

_____

_____

_____

_____

_____

_____

PROTECTION

From the time our children are born, we instinctively do all we can to protect them from harm. We were able to control their environment to protect them. Then, as they venture off to school or daycare, we realize we can't be there all the time to protect them. As parents of adult children, we know we can't protect them, although we may still want to. We want to protect them from the consequences of poor choices, hurts, illness, etc. We may try to offer some protection through words of caution and advice. but ultimately, they will make their own choices. (Psalms 91:5; NIV) reads, "If you say, 'The Lord is my refuge, and you make the Most High your dwelling, no harm will overtake you, no disaster will come near your tent.'" God is able to protect his children.

We all have to go through trials as we are warned in his word. Some trials are from God, some from Satan, and some created by ourselves from our actions. The trial may be difficult, but be encouraged, good is coming. God can bring positive results from those trials as he helps us grow to be more like him. Meditate on the wonderful promises God has for us in his word. (Psalms 112:1-2; NIV) "Praise the Lord! How blessed is the man who fears the Lord, who greatly delights in his commandments. His descendants will be mighty on earth; the generation of the upright will be blessed." Our children will be mighty on the earth! They will be blessed! Be patient with your children; they may need time to grow through their own trials. Let God's word give you hope and encouragement.

> (Psalms 91:14; NIV) "Because he loves me," says the Lord, "I will rescue him; I will protect him, for he acknowledges my name."

> (Proverbs 2:8; NIV) "...for he guards the course of the just and protects the way of his faithful ones."

> (Psalms 5:11; NLT) "But let all who take refuge in you rejoice; let them sing joyful praises forever. Spread your protection over them, that all who love your name may be filled with joy."

> (Psalms 25:21; NLT) "May integrity and honesty protect me, for I put my hope in you."

(Numbers 6:24-26: NLT) "May the Lord bless you and protect you. May the Lord smile on you and be gracious to you. May the Lord show you his favor and give you his peace."

(Psalms 32:7; NLT) "You are my hiding place; you protect me from trouble. You surround me with songs of victory."

Prayer: Lord, we are so thankful for your promises to protect our family. You are our loving Heavenly Father that sees and knows all that we do. You know our every thought. Nothing is hidden from you. We receive the comfort you have for us knowing you promise to protect those who acknowledge your name. We receive your peace knowing you watch over us and our family. Give our children wisdom and discernment. Lead them to a closer walk with you. We praise and thank you for rescuing, protecting and defending our family.

Meditation Moments:

_____

_____

_____

_____

_____

_____

_____

_____

_____

_____

SELF-CONTROL

Have you ever made New Year's resolutions to get into better shape? You go to the gym for a while until other things crop up, vying for your time and energy. Then, before you know it, your good intentions wane. Then those muscles you wanted to strengthen become weaker and less flexible. We can get weak spiritually as well, if we don't exercise some spiritual disciplines. Spiritual self-control takes effort, but one of the benefits is that it protects us from certain sins like pride, (Proverbs 25:27; NLT) and (Proverbs 16:32; NLT), gluttony (Proverbs 23:1-3; NIV), sexual sins (I Thessalonians 4:4; NIV) lying (Proverbs 17:20; NLT), and anger (Proverbs 29:11; NLT).

God also tells us to control our tongue (James 1:26-27; NIV), which is the most difficult of all. How many times have you opened your mouth, said things, and then wished you hadn't spoken? Our words can build up or tear down. (James 3:6; NIV) states our tongue can corrupt our whole body. (James 3:2; NLT) says if we control our tongue, we will be perfect and able to control ourselves in other ways. Controlling our tongue is a lifelong endeavor, but thanks be to God that we have a loving Father who gives us his Holy Spirit to empower us to be obedient. Let your words bring life to those around you today. No matter where you are in your struggle with self-control, our God is able to help you overcome.

> (Psalms 119:172; NLT) "Let my tongue sing about your word, for all your commands are right."

> (Romans 14:11; NIV) "'It is written: "As surely as I live,' says the Lord, 'every knee will bow before me; every tongue will acknowledge God'"'"

> (Psalms 34:12-13; NLT) "Does anyone want to live a life that is long and prosperous? Then keep your tongue from speaking evil and your lips from telling lies!"

> (Psalms 39:1; NLT) "I said to myself, "I will watch what I do and not sin in what I say. I will hold my tongue when the ungodly are around me."

(Proverbs 13:3; NLT) "Those who control their tongue will have a long life; opening your mouth can ruin everything."

(Proverbs 21:23; NLT) "Watch your tongue and keep your mouth shut, and you will stay out of trouble."

Prayer: Lord, as David said in (Psalms 141:3; NIV), "Set a guard over my mouth, Lord; keep watch over the door of my lips." Help me to exercise self-control in all areas, but especially with my words. I pray my words speak life, bring hope and encouragement to those around me. Thank you for helping me grow in this area to become more like you.

Meditation Moments:

_____

_____

_____

_____

_____

_____

_____

_____

_____

STORMS

Jesus calms the storms! Do thoughts from trials rage through your mind, tossing and turning like a violent storm? Jesus can calm the storms inside of us as easily as he did when he was in the boat with his disciples. Imagine what it was like in that boat. The disciples who were traveling with Jesus were fearful. In (Mark 4:37-40; NIV), "A furious squall came up, and the waves broke over the boat, so that it was nearly swamped. Jesus was in the stern, sleeping on a cushion. The disciples woke him and said to him, "Teacher, don't you care if we drown? He got up, rebuked the wind and said to the waves, "Quiet! Be Still!" Then the wind died down and it was completely calm. He said to his disciples, "Why are you so afraid? Do you still have no faith?"

So, what can you do while you're in the middle of a storm? How can you help your children that are going through storms in their life? Remember that he has given us the faith we need to believe he will see us through. (Luke 17:6; NIV) If you have the faith of a mustard seed you can move mountains.

When you focus on the problems, you invite fears to swamp you. Instead, put your trust in God's promises. Look to Jesus to calm you. Tell your heart, "Be quiet! Be still! God is in control!" Meditate on his word, sing psalms and hymns, think of all the things you can be thankful for, pray, rejoice…whatever it takes to switch the focus from fear to peace and calm.

> (Psalms 37:40; NLT) "The Lord helps them, rescuing them from the wicked. He saves them, and they find shelter in him."

> (Romans 8:26; NLT) "And the Holy Spirit helps us in our weakness. For example, we don't know what God wants us to pray for. But the Holy Spirit prays for us with groanings that cannot be expressed in words."

> (Proverbs 10:25; NIV) "When the storm has swept by, the wicked are gone, but the righteous stand firm forever."

(Ecclesiastes 7:14; NLT) "Enjoy prosperity while you can, but when hard times strike, realize that both come from God. Remember that nothing is certain in this life."

(Psalms 9:9; NLT) "The Lord is a shelter for the oppressed, a refuge in times of trouble."

Prayer: Lord, I give you my fears and doubts. Fill me with your peace during the storms. I know that nothing is too difficult for you. Help me to remember to keep my focus on you and not focus on the problems. Give me the wisdom and insight I need during these trials. Show me how I can help my children while they are going through a storm. I will put my trust in you. Thank you for your promises to give us comfort. I receive it by faith in the name of Jesus.

Meditation Moments:

_____

_____

_____

_____

_____

_____

_____

_____

_____

TRUST

Do you trust God? We often put more trust into ourselves and our abilities than we do in our almighty God, our Creator. We know our own weaknesses and inability to change ourselves, yet we continue to trust ourselves before trusting God. (Psalms 62:8; NIV) "Trust in him at all times, you people; pour out your hearts to him, for God is our refuge."

Trusting God may not be easy when we are in the heat of a situation. However, there is no better time than during a trial to trust God. God's Word is full of his promises for those who trust him. He is not unaware of the situation you or your family are going through. You may not always see or feel his presence with you during a trial, but be assured He is always with you and working for your benefit. Do we need to build trust in the relationship with our children? Have words or situations torn down the walls of trust in your family? (Romans 10:11; NIV) ""As scripture says, "Anyone who believes in him will *never* be put to shame.""

God has not closed his eyes to your tears and prayers. Meditate on what trust is. God's word is full of examples of his faithfulness and is well-deserving of our trust. Ask him to help you trust him more. Ask him to show you how you can build trust in your relationship with your children. Look up scriptures about trust. Most Bibles have a concordance in the back to help you locate some scriptures on trust. Ask God for wisdom to show you what you can do during this time as you trust him.

> (Jeremiah 17:7; NLT) "But blessed are those who trust in the Lord and have made the Lord their hope and confidence."

> (Isaiah 26:3; NLT) "You will keep in perfect peace all who trust in you, all whose thoughts are fixed on you!"

> (Romans 15:13; NIV) "May the God of hope fill you with all joy and peace as you trust in him, so that you may overflow with hope by the power of the Holy Spirit."

> (Psalms 9:10; NIV) "Those who know your name trust in you, for you, Lord, have never forsaken those who seek you."

(Romans 9:33; NIV) ""As it is written: "See, I lay in Zion a stone that causes people to stumble and a rock that makes them fall, and the one who believes in him will never be put to shame.""

Prayer: Lord, thank you for the work you are doing in my life and the lives of my loved ones. Help me to trust you more. Rebuild the trust within our family. Heal us of any past hurts that may have kept us from completely trusting in you. You have so many wonderful promises in your Word for those who trust in you. Thank you for giving us your Word to live and learn by. Because you are always faithful, I know I can put my trust in you.

Meditation Moments:

_____

_____

_____

_____

_____

_____

_____

_____

_____

WAITING

This is probably one of the hardest topics to implement. We live in such an instant society with instant access to almost anything. Few people practice patience. If we have to wait two minutes for our computer to boot, wait for a traffic light to change, wait in line at a store or wait on hold on the phone, we get impatient. Time in God's economy is totally different than ours. We don't seem to consider that as we rush through our days. He sees the 'big picture'. When we, or our children, are going through trials, he already knows the final outcome. We want our kids' problems to be 'fixed' by God NOW.

We don't want to wait. We want all the pain and hurt we are feeling to stop immediately. At some point, they will reach a place where they will have to choose for themselves to come to know God through a personal relationship and walk right before him. (Psalms 27:14; NLT) "Wait patiently for the Lord. Be brave and courageous. Yes, wait patiently for the Lord."

What can we do while we wait? We can continue to lift them up in prayer, trusting God to move in his perfect timing as he prepares their heart. Ask God to help you to be patient while he is working in their lives. God can bring complete healing of our hurts, restoration of relationships, and peace to our broken hearts. Nothing is too difficult for him.

It could be that the trial is part of their growing and learning process. Think back to experiences in your life that shaped you into a better a person? Those life lessons shape us into the adults we are. Our children need people who are on their side, who will patiently wait for them to get through their life lessons. We can't rush those lessons. Knowing you are on their side cheering them on can be a blessing to them. God has plans for them, to give them hope and a future. Let's patiently pray and watch God move in their lives.

> (Psalms 5:3; NIV) "In the morning, Lord, you hear my voice; in the morning I lay my requests before you and wait expectantly."

> (Ecclesiastes 7:8; NIV) "The end of a matter is better than its beginning, and patience is better than pride."

(Isaiah 30:18; NLT) "So the Lord must wait for you to come to him so he can show you his love and compassion. For the Lord is a faithful God. Blessed are those who wait for his help."

(Psalms 33:20; NIV) "We wait in hope for the Lord; he is our help and our shield."

Prayer: Lord, thank you for the wonderful work you are doing in the lives of my children. Although I don't always see what is happening I can be assured you heard me from my very first prayer. I know you are at work. Help me to patiently wait as I continue to learn to trust you more. Thank you for your patience with me as you continue your work in me. I will patiently wait and rejoice in the work you are doing. I will put my trust in your faithfulness.

Meditation Moments:

_____

_____

_____

_____

_____

_____

_____

_____

_____

_____

WISDOM

The Bible has a lot to say about wisdom. God values wisdom more than silver or gold. (Proverbs 16:16; NIV) states "How much better to get wisdom than gold, to get insight rather than silver!"

Certainly, having wisdom when dealing with kids is invaluable. So how does one go about to get more wisdom? In (II Chronicles 1:11-12; NIV), Solomon asked for wisdom and God blessed him more than anyone else in history because he asked for wisdom and not other things. In (Colossians 2:2-3; NIV), we are told that in Christ is hidden all the treasures of wisdom and knowledge. The Apostle Paul prayed for wisdom. (Ephesians.1:17; NIV) "I keep asking that the God of our Lord Jesus Christ, the glorious Father, may give you the Spirit of wisdom and revelation, so you may know him better." Paul's letter to Timothy (II Tim 3:15-17; NIV) tells how Timothy's learning of the scriptures since he was a child were able to make him wise for salvation through faith in Christ Jesus.

Another benefit of wisdom is that it helps you bring joy to others. (Proverbs 29:3; NIV) "The man who loves wisdom brings joy to his father..." Wisdom will bring joy to you. (Proverbs 3:13; NLT) "Joyful is the person who finds wisdom, the one who gains understanding."

Ask God for wisdom to better relate with your children. Ask God to give your children wisdom for their lives. Your Heavenly Father loves you and them. He wants you to have better relationships. He will give you the wisdom you need to develop strong, loving relationships with your children.

> (Luke 7:35; NLT) "But wisdom is shown to be right by the lives of those who follow it."

> (Proverbs 2:6; NIV) "For the Lord gives wisdom; from his mouth comes knowledge and understanding."

> (James 1:5; NIV) "If any of you lacks wisdom, you should ask God, who gives generously to all without finding fault, and it will be given to you."

(Proverbs 19:8; NIV) "The one who gets wisdom loves life; the one who cherishes understanding will soon prosper."

(Matthew 7:24; NIV) "Therefore, everyone who hears these words of mine and puts them into practice is like a wise man who built his house on the rock."

Prayer: Lord, thank you for your promises to give us wisdom when we ask in faith. I pray for wisdom to discern how I can be the best parent I can be. Help me to have the wisdom to know the times I need to sit back and pray or when to offer a listening ear, or when to give a word of encouragement to my children. Thank you for being our perfect wise Father. Give my children wisdom in their lives to walk obediently before you, to walk with honesty and integrity, and to make wise choices with their health, relationships, finances and careers.

Meditation Moments:

BECOMING A CHRIST FOLLOWER

If you would like to have a personal relationship with Jesus Christ and accepts his free gift of salvation, then say the prayer below.

Lord, I realized that I am a sinner and in need of a savior.
I recognize that Jesus Christ died on the cross for my sins.
Please forgive me of all my sins.
I now want to change and live obediently for you.
Fill me with your Holy Spirit and help me in my walk with you.
In Jesus' name I pray.

INSPIRATIONAL BIBLE VERSES

Romans 3:23

Romans 6:23

Romans 5:8

Romans 10:9

John 1:12

I John 1:19

John 15:4-5

PRAYER TIPS

Pray in Jesus' name.

Begin with thanking God for your children.

Ask God for wisdom.

Ask God to show you how to pray for your children.

Ask God to show you what you can do.

Ask God to show you what you shouldn't be doing for them.

Expect God to give you a plan.

Expect God to give you wisdom.

Expect God to act.

PRAYERS FOR OUR CHILDREN

Pray...

They will love the Lord with all their heart, mind and strength.

They will spend time each day in prayer and reading the Bible.

They will love others more than themselves, beginning at home.

They will serve in the church and the community.

They will walk with honesty and integrity.

They will not be selfish and self-centered, but others minded.

They will be wise in their choices.

They will be wise in managing money.

They will be dependable and hard workers.

They will be wise in their use of time, wisely balancing time with God, family, work, and rest.

They will daily express their love to their spouse first, then children.

They will be good providers for their family.

They will be godly examples to their children.

They will teach their children to love God and others.

~~~~~~~~~

ABOUT THE AUTHOR

Lisa and her husband, Jim, blended 2 families with 6 children, ages 5 through 17. Over the years, living through a myriad of life and family challenges, Lisa learned to draw her strength from God and rely on the promises in His word.

Lisa worked for the City of West Melbourne Florida, as the Director of Information Technology.

Tragedy struck their family when their 16 year old son was killed in car accident. 8 years later, Lisa and her husband facilitated the GriefShare Support program to offer hope and encouragement to others who lost loved ones.

She founded the Space Coast Scleroderma Support Group. She facilitated that support group for 8 years offering support, education, and hope for those dealing with Scleroderma.

Lisa and her husband facilitate the Dave Ramsey, Financial Peace University classes at their church. Lisa works as a Professional Guardian. She is appointed by the Brevard County Circuit Court to assist elders that have been deemed incapacitated and are at risk of being exploited, abused or neglected. Lisa and her husband reside in Melbourne Florida and enjoy time with their family and 8 grandchildren.

Printed in the United States
By Bookmasters